MW01268849

COMMUNICATION SECRETS FOR A HEALTHY MARRIAGE

JEAN-CLAUDE LEVEQUE

COMMUNICATION SECRETS FOR A HEALTHY
MARRIAGE

First Printed in Great Britain by
Obex Publishing Ltd in 2020

1 2 4 6 8 10 9 7 5 3

Paperback ISBN: 978-1-913454-25-8
eBook ISBN: 978-1-913454-26-5

A CIP catalogue record for this book is available
from the British Library

Obex Publishing Limited
Reg. No. 12169917

CONTENTS

Introduction

Congratulations on purchasing *Communication Secrets For A Healthy Marriage,* and thank you for doing so.

The following chapters will discuss communication in marriages as the key to saving marriages. With millions of divorces recorded over time, surviving marriage has become a foreign aspect to most spouses. The era of technology and social media has made it harder to maintain spousal respect and communication in many marriages, making divorce a common aspect today.

In this handbook, you will get to learn the importance of communication in your marriage, the consequences of lacking communication, and tools that can help improve communication between you and your spouse. 90% of marital problems can be solved by merely communicating - Fact. Talking to your spouse about common issues, your fears and insecurities can help them know how you feel and give you more love and assurance.

The book also digs deep into aspects of a good talk. When speaking to your spouse, there's the art of listening and the art of speaking involved. Not knowing how to listen and comprehend, or how to speak with your spouse politely will cause a communication breakdown. Respecting your spouse is essential in communication and in a lasting marriage.

You can say so much without having to speak to each other; hence, the author visits the rules of taking a marital break to save your marriage and improve your communication skills.

There are plenty of books on this subject on the market, thanks again for choosing this one! Every effort was made to ensure it is full of as much useful information as possible, please enjoy!

Chapter 1:
The Difference Between a Healthy and Unhealthy Marriage

Ever met a couple that resembles perfection? Well, it is a reliable fact that most married couples don't. In the US alone, there were over 700000 registered divorces in the year 2018. With the increasing rate of divorces, it is safe to state that at least 50% of marriages will end in divorce.

There's nothing as painful as having friction with the one person with whom you promised a lifetime. There is also nothing as sad as having to act perfectly in public and trying to hold on to ashes. Therefore, in the coming chapters, you will get to learn several reasons that lead marriages to divorce. And how to prevent that from happening to your marriage.

Before you take a peek into an excellent example of a healthy marriage, here are a few signs of an

COMMUNICATION SECRETS FOR A HEALTHY
MARRIAGE
unhealthy marriage.

You don't seem to spend meaningful time anymore

During the honeymoon phase, you two love birds seemed inseparable. You wanted to go to the market together, go for trips offers, hang out with each other's families, spend every waking minute with each other and even eat from the same place and spoon. Nothing seemed better than being around each other, making love four times a day like a damn prescription. You probably irritated everyone around you with all your love and cuteness.

Today that doesn't seem to be the case. The neighbours never seem to see the two of you together unless it is Sunday and you have to drive to church in one car to put up a show. You do not spend meaningful time anymore, and making love, it's just sex. No passion, no feelings, no foreplay. It's more like, "okay, we're horny; let's get this over with." If it's really bad, you don't even touch each other anymore. A kiss doesn't seem familiar, and you can barely watch a movie in the same room. A conversation smells like a morgue, and you want to end it the minute it begins. Your phone and laptop are your new best friends.

Dinners are enjoyed separately and visiting the market solo is the most refreshing activity in your life. Your partner has stopped being your love, your life and your world. They are now the guy/girl in the living room. Even college roommates have more fun together. Maybe you do not feel all these, but you feel this kind of energy from your partner.

No more fights

Now, don't get this wrong. Your relationship should not be filled with battles all day and night, no. However, remember s marriage is made up of two different personalities. It does not matter if you have a hundred things in common; there are a hundred more personality differences yet to discover as you live together. The small things like the toilet seat, to big things like how to raise children, will cause friction and result in frequent arguments. So that is normal.

But here you are in a *silent* marriage. No arguments, no fights, one of you seems to be brushing off every detail and appears to agree with everything the other says, without putting up a fight. Lacking fights in a marriage, (please note that fights stand for verbal altercations and not physical confrontations) means that one of you is tired and done. One of you has given up trying to find commonalities. Whether you like your partner's ideas or not, your responses will always be, "okay" or "whatever you say". This means you do not care, and you will not bother.

This phase is usually a sign of a dead marriage, and in most cases, the love is not revivable. It means that one, or both of you, have tried and come to the conclusion that your marriage cannot be saved, so you gave up, and now you are just existing or "surviving".

It's their fault

There is no way on this green earth that your partner is at fault 100% if the time and you are off the hook for everything that caused an argument between you two. You must have played a part in it Maybe your partner made a mistake, but then perhaps it is your fault they that small issue escalated into a sleepless night. Take an example; your partner gets home late. He or she did not give you a heads up that they will be late. The minute the front door opens, you start to shout and accuse them of infidelity and dishonesty, or secrets too.

Now, no one is saying that what your partner did is right, but your reaction was wrong as well. Therefore, as your partner apologizes, do not keep hammering, apologize for the adverse reaction as well. Unfortunately, in an unhealthy relationship, either both parties will not apologize, or one will act perfect and fault the other.

There is verbal and physical abuse

As earlier mentioned, misunderstandings due to different personalities are usual. They are also healthy for they help you learn each other more and in turn grow as a couple. Now, these fights become a red flag when they turn into verbal abuse or physical abuse.

Insulting a partner is wrong; it does not matter how small the insults are. Once you show your partner that it is okay to send "small" insults your way, then they will be comfortable to throw more copious insults at you in the future. And if you embrace them too, then kicks and blows are around the corner.

If your relationship becomes abusive (whether verbally or physically), then it is unhealthy and it is time to do something about it.

And then there were two different personalities

As you can term this as being bipolar or having dissociative identity disorder, sometimes it is just stress or depression, say one of you drinks alcohol. During that drunken state, they become abusive to the other. On the same note, your partner may get deep into drinking more often and succumb to alcoholism. In some cases, after your partner drinks, they reveal intense emotions on the scale of breaking down, crying, opening up and much more. All those "drunk personalities" flip when the person gets sober. Maybe it is not alcohol, and perhaps they have one personality when in private and a different one when in public. It does not necessarily have to be good and bad, respectively, maybe it is the vice versa.

When a partner showcases different personalities, it means that they are bottling up stress from the marriage or work or other environments and only react in situations or environments that seem mentally safe for them.

While the reactions may not be abusive, it is still a

red flag to your marriage, and it may be time to address the issue with a professional or together as a couple. However, if they are physically abusive, it may be in your best interest to walk out of the marriage.

Secrets and lies

Your partner does not have to lie or keep secrets on infidelity for it to be a red flag to your marriage. Say they are secretive about health matters, work, and their family and such. Even as a married couple, you still live two lives, hence sometimes things happen in your life that is not happening in your partner's life.

Remember the vow, "through the good times and bad?" Well, the bad times are here, and the promises have become invalid. No matter what goes on in your personal (separate) lives, a healthy marriage is whereby you approach each other, discuss the issues together and try to find solutions as one.

When your partner opts for secrets and lies, then your marital bond broke, you're no longer their pillar, and they do not trust to tell you their problems. Sometimes they are just scared if your reactions and sometimes they are trying to protect you. But secrets and lies are just that.

The unhealthy list could go on and in, but the mentioned are the most common. If you are experiencing any of the listed situations, then your marriage is on the rocks and needs some repair. Relationships change continuously over time, and sometimes one partner grows faster or differently from the other. This makes communication essential to remaining on the same page in the journey of spending a lifetime together.

KEY SECRETS TO A HEALTHY MARRIAGE

What is a healthy marriage? It is one that is not perfect but tries to be. It is never really about being perfect, and anyway, perfect is relative. As a couple, you have your own goals, achieving those emotional and financial goals are gaining perfection. A lot is required to remain on the right path of a healthy marriage and the efforts expected from both partners.

Sexual faithfulness

Talk about being faithful to your partner. Infidelity ranges from the body to mind, eyes and lips. So, do not limit yourself to doing everything but sex. Kissing is wrong and desiring another human being is also cheating. Your mind, body and soul should belong to your spouse.

Humility

Nothing beats humility in a life of relations, no matter the type of relationship. Being able to take the high road, institute a conversation even when your spouse is the one at fault, is a rare maturity. Fortunately, being human enough to accept correction or relate to a situation will save your marriage in the long run. In most cases, your humility inspires your spouse character, and they might learn to be humble as well. When your spouse sees you readily accepting mistakes and allowing corrections, then doing the same will be a party for them because they know you can relate.

Patience and Forgiveness

On the same, not be patient with your spouse when

they seem to be going through a tough time. Sometimes a spouse keeps secrets from you to tell you when they are comfortable. Don't rush them and make them withdraw from you. Show the support and be patient; they will open up. Then forgive them for taking the time to open up. Forgive your spouse for the little things they do. More often than not, your character towards your spouse can either build them or break them. Forgiving them when they least expect it will help them view life from a different perspective and appreciate you more for giving them a chance. Now when it is your turn to be shown patience and be forgiven, your spouse will do so without hesitation.

Honesty and trust

Without these two features in your marital foundation, your relationship will not go far. As you wait upon your spouse to practice honesty, be ready to show trust. It is a two-way street. Also, be honest with your spouse, even when honesty seems like a tough decision. What if honesty will ruin our relationship? You may ask.

Well, the answer is simple. Do not do things that

will harm your marriage, and you will not need to be dishonest about your toxic information.

Communication

Talk about it all. The good, the bad, the funny, the sad. Nothing should be off-limits. To have a healthy relationship, being able to communicate your feelings and fears will help you understand each other better even as you grow, you will be able to do so in unison because of communication. This handbook will explain different aspects of communication and how to go about them.

Chapter 2:

Importance of Communication in Marriages

How married people share their agenda is very crucial to their success and quality of the marriage. Most couples underestimate the importance of communication in their marriages. They think that the daily banter or lack of it does not have a long term effect on their marriage, but it does. All the critical issues are passed on through effective communication. You need to express your emotions adequately so your partner can understand what is going on and how you can tackle the issue together.

Expressing yourself to your partner is a practice that should be followed from the dating stage so that it can become the cornerstone of your marriage. Most of the marriage characteristics, such as trust, honesty, love, are expressed through communication. Practising proper communication, whether verbal or non-verbal, is key to a healthy marriage.

Life may get hectic, therefore denying couples the chance to have deep conversations. Lack of these conversations will make you feel lonely and sad even though you are with your partner. Discussed below are some of the advantages that come with communication in marriages that will give you the initiative to work on your communication skills with your significant other.

Saves you money

Flowers, chocolates and other gifts are well known as offers when a spouse has made a mistake and is seeking an apology. Errors made when a spouse has said the wrong thing or has just failed to say the right thing. Having deep and regular conversations with your spouse helps you to understand them more in-depth. You get to know what they like and what they do not. You can also tell what they want to hear and more natural ways to relay information to them. Buying these gifts frequently can get expensive. However, frequent conversations will reduce the rate of mistakes and arguments you have with your spouse hence saving you money.

Saves time

Taking time to understand what your spouse is trying to explain to you will help you save a lot of time in future. Take your time to solve issues that were pending will be of help since you will not have to revisit issues or explain anything again. When talking to your spouse, make sure to go into detail about all the problems that you want them to get acquainted. When you have passed your point clearly, and they understand everything you said, it will be easier to know what you want. It saves time since there will be fewer questions asked during future conversations and fewer arguments since the information you passed before was transparent and honest. Clear communications, when conducted at one moment, will save time for future conversations instead of repeating the same issues over and over.

Good for your health

Stress is a common issue among married couples. In-depth conversations with your significant other will help in reducing stress. Stress in a marriage is reducible in two ways. One is by reducing tension. Unresolved issues between you and your spouse can cause anxiety since you will not know what your partner is thinking or doing. This tension can cause you to be unsettled and irritable, therefore affecting your social and mental health. Communication between the two of you will set things straight and thus reduce the tension. You will, therefore, know what your spouse is thinking or what they plan on doing, which will help you to be more relaxed and calm.

Secondly, communication reduces stress by allowing spouses to vent to each other. Anxiety and uncertainties can be airing when couples communicate. Through venting, couples tell each other everything that may be bugging them in one way in another. The issues can be about your significant other or other aspects of life. Venting helps to come to an agreement as a couple and also try to solve the different problems outside marriage as a team by sharing ideas. Addressing the issues affecting your marriage as a team will strengthen the bond between you two and keep you mentally stable.

You can focus on other things

Often you will find yourself continuing conversations you had earlier with your spouse in your head. Thinking of wittier or better answers, you should have used in an argument is very common. You spend a lot of time thinking about arguments you had with your partner, how there are better words you should use, a point you did not pass across or on who was right or wrong. During such periods a lot of the time that you should spend being productive is spent on thinking about marriage issues which can cause you to be distracted hence less productive. Solving all your problems in one sitting will allow you to focus more on other things since you will not be thinking about scenarios that would change what happened earlier, therefore, making you more productive.

It strengthens the relationship

Communication is the fuel of any relationship. Communicating with anyone is likely to make them understand you more and learn about your expectations and aspirations. You learn more about a person when you hear them talk about their experiences, likes and dislikes. When you communicate effectively, people can align their ambitions and lifestyles to yours. It also weeds out people with whom you may not be compatible with hence making it easier for everyone to move with the right people through life. The same applies to marriage.

Constant and meaningful communication makes you understand your spouse more and more each time you talk to each other. You get to know what they are fascinated about of late and what interests them. You are also able to pick up hints they leave whether intentionally or unintentionally. It makes it easier to plan for the future and understand your partners love language easier. Lack of communication causes the relationship to wither for lack of excitement. It may cause couples to lose interest in each other and even become strangers since people keep developing daily. Constant communication is proof to ensure the relationship lasts longer and healthy.

You learn more about yourself

The ability to change your thoughts to words forces you to clarify them so that the person you are talking to can understand. Continued communication enables you to fine-tune your ideas.

COMMUNICATION SECRETS FOR A HEALTHY MARRIAGE

The more you practice your communication skills, the more you become competent. It sharpens your skills, so you are more accurate to express yourself without diverting from your intended topic. The ability to clearly express yourself in marriage is crucial since it ensures your spouse does not have to guess what you want or what you are trying to communicate.

Passing the right information will reduce speculations and therefore make it easier for the two of you to come to an understanding. Listening to your spouse will make you learn more about things about yourself that irritate your spouse and that they may need you to change them. Listening will teach you about yourself, and you can decide on the things to adjust to accommodate your significant other and make it a happy marriage.

Less hassle

Avoiding communication may bring more problems than communication. Being silent comes with a lot of troubles such as pestering from your spouse, who may be wondering what they did wrong or why you are overly quiet. Staying quiet in such situations will make the pestering even worse and therefore ruin your peace of mind. Remaining silent may seem that you are in control of the situation, but in reality, it may bring about a spouse who is insecure and has trust issues.

Talking with your significant other will reduce the pressure that comes with such situations and make things easier for both of you. Taking time to communicate may seem like a hassle, but it is likely to solve more problems that may come in future. It reduces the questions, uncertainties and clarification that will be needed in future since the conversations held will straighten things out. Reduced pestering from your partner will make your marriage life more comfortable and therefore, healthy marriage in the long run

It is a chance to learn

People develop daily. Each day comes with its unique challenges, lessons and experiences. We also meet different people daily who may teach us something different, whether directly or indirectly.

Communication is the easiest way to learn a thing or two from different people. Your spouse had a whole life before meeting you. They had an entire childhood and have met a lot of different people before finally meeting you.

Details of these past experiences are released gradually since they are rooted in memory and cannot come out at once. Communication with your significant other may make it easier to learn more about their past experiences and understand more about the person they were before meeting you. Spending time with them and participating in activities is also likely to trigger memories about related events that happened in the past which they can share to enable you to learn more about them. Creating time for communication with your partner may teach you something new that they have learned recently or an experience that happened to them in the past.

Makes it easier in future

Being able to have a fruitful conversation to completion creates confidence for future discussions.

Once you and your significant other conduct one complete conversation, you will be yearning for future conversations that have a success rate like that of the previous one. It builds a stepping stone to the other discussions, and since you seem to have the secret to performing the conversations, it will be easier for you to have the same type of communications. The success record creates motivation for future successes on the same.

Reduces the number of arguments

You do not have to wait for the major case for you to communicate with your significant other. Many factors are essential in a marriage such as finances, hygiene and behaviour in general. It is vital to discuss these matters now and then when an issue comes up. It ensures the small arguments are solved before they turn into a significant discussion. Ignoring the problems may seem like a viable solution, but it only works temporarily. Setting aside time to handle the matters is the most effective way to ensure all issues solved in the right time, and therefore you are both happy in the marriage.

It is fun

COMMUNICATION SECRETS FOR A HEALTHY MARRIAGE

Communicating with the love of your life is a fun activity for both of you. You can ask everything that you think is complicated and that you feel your significant other can answer. You can explore the other person's mind to know how they think and answer all your childhood questions and curiosity you had about the other gender. You can incorporate other activities that you feel can help you communicate easily where both of you will enjoy while also expressing yourself to your significant other. You can even create a routine for you where you have set aside a specific time for communication where you link it with other activities to make it more fun and increase its chances of success.

Having challenges in marriage is typical to all couples. You should not be worried since it is nothing that cannot be solved. Making adjustments in areas that you think cause problems in your communication is a step in the right direction. Accepting that there is a problem and searching for means to solve it is the first step to solving any problem. Changes made in communication do not have to be drastic; small changes made will have a high impact in the future as compared to no change made at all.

Small, consistent steps in communication will help to improve your relationships in general, and you will understand your spouse better and express yourself better so it can be easier to solve your differences and come to an agreement. Understanding the advantages that come with proper communication in a marriage will help you strive to improve the communication between you and your partner to ensure you have a healthy marriage.

Chapter 3:

Communication Tools to use in your Marriage

People have different styles of communication. If your method of communication matches that of your spouse, then you are in luck since it is easier for you to communicate, and therefore you agree faster. However, the majority of the population are couples whose styles of communication and the complete opposite or are not fully compatible. The most distinctive methods of communication are a passive style, which are people who are verbal processors. These types of people tend to think as they talk. The delivery of information is done passively using words that will not offend or cause an extreme reaction to the person they are talking to. This type of communication use perfectly packaged words and phrases to appeal to their audience.

The other type of communication is processing information internally first, then using the director method. This type of communication involves thinking before talking and delivering the information directly so that the intended recipient does not misinterpret it. Realizing your kind of communication will make you self-aware, and you can even start to gauge the type of communication that your partner uses. When the communication styles are different, it is common for confusion to arise where you may not know what your spouse is trying to say.

Failure to understand each other causes frustrations and makes it even harder to communicate more. To solve such problems, we came up with tools you can incorporate in your conversations for easy understanding as a couple. Using these tools will also help you in overcoming your differences and solve any conflicts with ease.

The creative number technique

Using this tool, you make it easy to make a decision. It makes it easier to clarify what you are saying by assigning numbers to possible answers; therefore, more comfortable with making a decision. It shows how important an issue is to your spouse and can, therefore, make it easier to make a decision based on

how she feels. An example of how you use this
method is as below:

- I am not interested in this
- I am not interested in this, but I can talk
  about it
- I do not care
- I am interested in doing it, but it will not
  hurt if we don't
- Yes I am interested

Choosing a number can work as a simple answer
about how your spouse feels towards a particular
subject.

The pencil method

With this method, you use a pencil. If you do not
have a pencil, you can improvise and use anything
that you can hold. The person in possession of the
pencil gets the chance to talk. Meanwhile, the other
person may get an opportunity to ask clarifying
questions on matters concerning the issue, but that
is all.

This method is effective because it gives you and
your partner equal opportunities to talk. When it is
your chance to talk, you should try and express your

feelings while being as honest as possible. Explain to your partner how you feel and feel entirely vulnerable. It should work since there will be no interruptions from your partner who, in other cases, can try to be defensive or interrupt you while you talk.

While holding the pencil, you need to say everything that you want to say then pass the pencil to your partner. When your partner has the pencil, the same rules that applied to them now apply to you. To get started, you can flip a coin since it gives both of you an equal opportunity without favours.

Some of the arguments can be too hot to handle. In these cases, you can get a third party who can act as a mediator or get a therapist when the issues get too hot to handle. Seeking help from other parties may appear as a sign of weakness, but in reality, it is a sign of strength since it shows a sense of responsibility and that you care for your marriage.

The fifteen minutes time out rule

This method has a lot of similarities to the pencil rule. However, in this method, instead of passing over a pencil to exchange talking opportunities, you give your partner fifteen minutes of silence as they talk about their feelings. When in the heat of the moment during an argument, you can say mean hurtful things that can scar your spouse's feelings. To avoid lashing out at each other, you can make use of this trick.

Give your partner fifteen minutes of silence and allow them to speak their minds freely without interrupting. When fifteen minutes are over, they should be finishing with what they had to say and give you your fifteen minutes to talk. The chance of speaking without interruptions allows you to clearly express how you feel and therefore make it easier to solve your differences.

The H.A.L.T method.

This method focuses on the correct timing when intending to pass information to your spouse. Choosing the right timing to deliver the information is a sure way to ensure your partner listens well and understands what you want to tell them. You should halt yourself from talking about important matters when one of you feels, Hungry, Angry, Lonely, or Tired. Experiencing any of the feelings can cause an argument to go completely wrong.

Whenever you get any of these feelings, you need to stop arguing immediately and attend to them. You can go on with the argument after you have gotten rid of the atmosphere. The feelings can inhibit you or your partner from listening to the discussion. Dealing with the feeling is supposed to give you time to think about what your partner was talking about. Put it into consideration as you also assess your views so you can come to a better understanding with your partner.

The S.T.O.P strategy

In this method, S.T.O.P is an acronym that stands for Stop, Time out, Own your own part, Peace offering. Every letter is assigned a role during arguments. For Stop, you need to halt the conversation when you do not like the direction it is taking. It will give you a break to think before going on with the conversation. Time out gives you a chance to physically separate for 30 to 60. It gives you a chance to calm down and recollect yourself before you do on with the discussion.

Own your own part; this part insists that everyone should own their role in being part of the problem. You should be able to admit to your mistakes

instead of pressuring your partner. Owning your part
of the errors will quickly solve your issues and show
that you take full responsibility for your actions.
Peace offering, this happens when the discussion is
over. It acts as a ritual to celebrate the successful
completion of the conversation. You shared what
you have learned and how you can have a change of
behavior to prevent future issues. You can decide to
seal the deal with a kiss or your preferred way of
celebration.

The pause principle

It is a strategy on how to deal with your discussions.
Its main aim is to ensure the conversation does not
become a heated argument and ensures it remains in
control. PAUSE, in this case, stands for. Prepare,
Affirm, Understand, Search, Evaluate. The first step
before beginning the discussion is preparation. In
this stage, you need to get your facts right and
develop options with which you can use to control
the conversation. The second step is an affirmation.
Here you should show genuine love and affirm to
your partner that you love them, and you will keep
respecting them.

You should then understand different interests.

Your partner may have different needs, desires, concerns, or even limitations. You need to acknowledge that you are aware, and you understand that they can be different from you, but all that matters is the love that you share. You should then evaluate every argument passed reasonably. Take your time to get into your partner's shoes and understand the issues from their perspective. Analyze the options and apologize where necessary.

The discussed above are just a few of the common tricks that you can use to make conversations easier in your marriage. People can have different communication tactics that make it hard to get along, but including one or two tips regularly is bound to make your marriage life more comfortable and more enjoyable.

Chapter 4:

Effects of a Lack of Communication in Marriages

You become emotionally distant

Communication creates a connection between you and your spouse. It helps to know what your significant other has been up to so you can catch up. The lack of communication creates a rift between the two of you hence becoming emotionally distant. The lack of communication and the distance created between the two of you can cause love to fade away. Lack of communication comes with the lack of joy in marriage, such as less inclination to sex, doing shared activities, or the drive to solve the marriage problems. It can lead to loss of love and even divorce. Your significant other may be refusing to talk due to the silent treatment, partner criticism, or as a defensive tactic. Trying to solve these problems and creating an environment where you can freely talk with your partner will make it easy to

JEAN-CLAUDE
LEVEQUE

communicate and air out their opinions.

Results in wrong assumptions

When you do not communicate effectively with your significant other, therefore are bound to make assumptions since they cannot get the right information that they require. Most assumptions made by your partner may not be correct. They may think that you are cheating on them or doing anything that will affect them negatively. Once the process of making assumptions begins, partners are likely to make more. They are expected to associate every action that you make to other assumptions. Therefore when doing anything, it is essential to explain to your partner the reason for it so that they can understand your point of view and thus reduce the rate of assumptions they create. The assumptions made will destroy the relationship since your partner will be stressed out and may lose their trust in you. The best way to reduce assumptions is by clearing the air every time.

Your sex life suffers

Lack of communication brings about frustrations

even in your sex life. The absence of the desired sex can cause disappointments and frustrations due to one partner not getting an orgasm. Lack of communication on such issues can cause hostility and distress on your partner since they are not able to express themselves and state the problems affecting your sex life. Being open with one another leads to a beautiful sex life because anyone can initiate the first move, and your significant other can be open to experimentation. Sex is a crucial part of marriage life. For both of you to enjoy it, you need to discuss it in detail, such as the frequency, fantasies, and turn-ons. Honesty, when talking about your expectations during sex will help your partner to be aware of their role during sex so that you can both enjoy and have a more fulfilling sex life.

No communication means no compromise

Nobody is always right. For your relationship to be perfect, it should have a foundation of trust, obedience, and agreement. Balance is an essential aspect of marriage because you and your significant other need to compromise and come to an equilibrium decision that works for both of you. Communication creates a platform where you can both share your views and compromise on the issues. Failure to agree on any subject can seem to deny your partner their rights and come off as unfair. It can make your partner lose your trust in you and see the marriage as a dishonest relationship. Being able to compromise and accommodate your partner's view and believes will make them feel comfortable in the relationship, therefore, building love and trust.

You seek others to fill the void

Failure to communicate effectively in a marriage can turn you into roommates and strangers. Isolating your spouse in your thoughts and actions will make them feel alone and lonely. It may cause them to seek another person who will make them feel wanted and loved. Spouses may need validation from time to time. Lack of validation will make them crave it and therefore look for it in a different place. Lack of proper communication may cause your partner to feel insecure and therefore look for someone else out of the marriage to fill the void that they feel is present in the marriage. Proper communication, however, creates a loving environment and make your spouse feel validated in every way.

Chapter 5:

Types of Communication in Marriage

Optical communication

It is the type of communication shared by seeing. It occurs when you see another person and notice their presence, and also they see you and notice your presence. It involves noticing your partner and getting the details such as the clothes they chose to wear the hairstyle they have and their body type. After an analysis of what you see, you decide whether you like what you see or not. When you like what you see, you can go to the next step, which is finding a way to let your partner know. If you are not impressed, you can ignore or find a decent way to criticize it.

Optical communication is the first type of communication that attracted you to your spouse in the first place. It is from this type of communication that you form the first judgments you make, and also you get to create a first impression. Tastes are also seen first through seeing. Incorporating your partners taste in your appearance can give you bonus points since they will know that you listen to them and that this opinion matters to you.

Optical communication is essential in marriage because if you can please your spouse with how you look, it will keep them attracted to you and therefore fall in love with you more. Optical communication is also how other people, such as your friends, communicate first—presenting yourself as a loving couple shows other people that you are in love and that you respect each other.

Auditory communication

It is the communication shared through listening. In a marriage, it can be considered the best way to communicate since it gives you a lot of information that you can use to know more about your partner and what they like. Listening to your partner when they speak shows that you love them, and you enjoy the conversations that you have with them. Also, when people listen to your discussions, it makes you feel appreciated and loved. It will give you the confidence to express yourself more in the future

hence making conversations more comfortable. It
also gives you the freedom to vent since you are sure
to find a listening ear when you need one.

Auditory communication helps you to make a
connection with someone on a more intimate level.
You get to understand their feelings and how they
think. From the information you gather from
auditory communication, you can use it to judge and
make a decision on how you are going to respond. A
lot of information is consumable through this type
of communication, whether knowingly or
unknowingly. It is, therefore, wise to pick the words
you use so that you do not mislead them or give
them the wrong information that may cause harm to
our marriage. Excellent auditory communication is
essential for every marriage since it is the main
avenue of communication.

Emotional communication

It always used to communicate with people on a
more intimate level. Relationships come with
emotions. The emotional connection allows people
to express themselves into detail on how the
information you provided has affected them and

JEAN-CLAUDE
LEVEQUE

how they feel rather than the superficial response that you can get from everyone. Emotional communication involves analysis of a situation, then reacting to it intelligently while considering your partner's feelings. Showing emotions is part of being human. You should, therefore, be free to show emotions, especially to your spouse, since it shows that you are open around them and can express yourself to them freely.

It shows that you trust them, and therefore you can be honest around them. For example, if your partner informs you that their childhood pet has passed on, you should be able to show emotions to them since it is something that sad and, therefore, a sad mood used. Emotional communication involves receiving and being able to manage their feelings. Sometimes the emotions in play can be overwhelming. However, you should be able to assess the situation and give honest feedback while still maintaining the emotions to encourage your partner and assure them that you have their back.

Nonverbal communication

It is a type of interaction that involves all cues rather

than voice-related ones. These cues show your partner's reaction even before the verbal answer can follow it. Examples of non-verbal communication are facial expressions and body language. You can tell a lot about a person by observing their body language as you talk to them. Even without them incorporating verbal communication, you can tell your partner's reaction to anything based on their body language.

Reactions exhibited on body language show that your partner is attentively listening, and that is why they show the responses. Using these cues, you can assess the direction the conversation is taking and know whether your spouse is in agreement, or they are against what you are saying. Learning to read nonverbal communication is essential since it will guide you on how to handle your conversations. For example, when saying something to your spouse and you notice them frowning at you. It shows that they dislike the point you are trying to put across and are likely to go against it.

Verbal communication

It involves communicating through phrases and sentences vocally to create dialogue. However, verbal communication is not just about putting words together so they can form a sentence. You need to be able to develop a sensible sentence that can relay the information you intend to pass efficiently so that it is understandable. When talking to your partner, you need to include all types of communication so that you can know their reaction based on what you are saying. Studying how they react as you speak will give you the go-ahead or a stop sign on when to terminate a conversation or have a change of topic.

Choosing words that resonate well with your spouse will likely lead to a fruitful conversation since both of you will enjoy participating in it. Verbal communications are susceptible. You need to choose your words well so that your partner can understand what you are trying to put across without offending them and also so that you can achieve your desired results. Verbal communication is essential in marriage since it is the most eloquent way you can express yourself and, therefore, clear things up before your partner comes up with assumptions that can ruin your marriage.

Chapter 6:

Typical Issues that cause a Communication Breakdown

Life gets in the way

When a relationship has been going on for a while, it starts to seem like a routine. If you and your spouse are both in the professional field, you can immerse yourself into the busy lifestyles that may cause you to ignore your partner unintentionally. Stress arising from jobs is an excellent example of how life can get in the way. The pressure from your job can be a result of conflicting work schedules or difficulties from your supervisor or colleagues. Other relationships are known to affect your marriage life. If you fail to get along well with your friends, family, or colleagues, the stress from those relationships is likely to be transferred and reflected in your intimate relationship.

When the stress or pressure from outside gets to

you, you are likely to internalize it or take it out on your spouse. Your significant other should serve as a person on your team. You should be able to confide in them so it can be a way to relieve the stress. However, when the pressure gets to you, it may seem like your spouse is among the reasons for the anxiety. The situation gets worse when children come in, and their needs should be a priority. It makes you unable to handle the stress, which hinders communication. Issues that arise from prioritization and time management are some of the problems that can cause a communication breakdown in the marriage.

No trust

For your marriage to be happy, it has to have a foundation of honesty and trust. Lack of these fundamental values is bound to have your partner to have troubles in communication. Creating trust is more comfortable than restoring it. When your partner loses their confidence in you, it will take a lot of time to repair it, and it can even lead to divorce. Your partner can lose their trust in you for different circumstances based on how they view you and what they believe. However, some of the common reasons that your significant other may lose trust in you are finance, in this case, your partner may feel that you are not transparent enough on how you spend your money. Infidelity, once you are unfaithful to your spouse, it is challenging to restore their trust. It causes a lot of pain and can damage your partner ultimately.

Lack of emotional intimacy. It occurs when you cannot trust your partner with your secrets. The secrets you have can be fears, hopes, or feelings. Lack of emotional intimacy in a marriage can cause your spouse to seek intimacy somewhere else, which can bring about trust issues in the marriage. For communication to be effective in a marriage, you will need to be very honest with each other and build your trust. Trust grows when there is continuous honesty and transparency between the two if you. With this, it will be easier for you to communicate with your spouse.

An external trauma or shock

Events outside your marriage life have a massive impact on how you behave in your marriage life. Shocks from outside events can cause you to carry the trauma you experienced from the events to your marriage. Bringing such issues can bring about difficulties when it is time to communicate with your significant other. The circumstances causing the shocks are such as severe illnesses or scares, loss or grief, an accident, redundancy, or loss of a job.

The mentioned are all events that can cause us trauma and therefore change us as a person in general. With the magnitude of how the events affect your brains. It will also affect how you communicate with your partner. Some of the situations are humiliating, which can, therefore, make you find it difficult to explain it to your spouse. Talking during traumatic events is challenging since you can even lack the right words to articulate yourself eloquently. You should always try your best to communicate with your partner when they are going through these hard times as a constant reminder to stay encouraged.

Lack of physical intimacy

Physical intimacy is essential in a marriage for bonding. The lack of this intimacy shows that there is a problem in your communication. A problem with physical intimacy causes the rise of other issues

which enhance the problem of communication.
Communicating about these issues will help you to
acknowledge that there is a problem that needs
solving. You can, therefore, find out the root cause
of the problem and thus go back to more physical
intimacy and better sex life in general. Lack of
communication will cause the problem to
deteriorate, further creating more marital issues.

Toxic behaviours

When your behaviour is toxic, it will likely lead to
an unhealthy relationship. As the marriage gets
toxic, it becomes harder to communicate due to the
refusal to change in behaviour. Toxic traits may
come from one partner or both. If the unhealthy
actions are not taken control over and combated,
you can be sure that they will affect the relationship
negatively. Some of the common toxic traits in
married couples are constant criticism. It happens
when you constantly criticize your partner's
personality instead of the behaviour.

It can get to them, and they may see them as hurtful
attacks. Stonewalling, this happens when partners
cannot share everything they are going through in

some cases, it may even lead to the spouse not talking to each other. It causes couples not to open up to each other, and you both keep bottling your feelings. Defensiveness is when partners decide to stick to their views with an unwillingness to change. It can be as a result of victimization from your partner. It can cause the conflict to persist since both of you are not willing to come up with a neutral solution.

Noticing these traits is the first step in conquering them. Breaking down these toxic habits will ease communication between you and your partner since you will both be willing to accept each other's views. Communicating about these traits and dealing with them as a team is also an excellent way to start and will improve the quality of your communication in general.

COMMUNICATION SECRETS FOR A HEALTHY
MARRIAGE

Chapter 7:

How to Improve your Communication Skills

Use respective listening

Lack of attention is among the significant causes of the breakdown of communication in your marriage. Once you notice it as a problem, you should choose to be the bigger person and accommodate the idea of respective listening. It involves being calm and listening through what your spouse has to say—and trying to understand their point of view.

Taking the initiative to start will cause a change in how your marital conversations go and therefore improving them in general. Waiting for your spouse to make the first move never works. It is also likely to haunt you more since you will keep noticing it every time you try to communicate with them. Offering respective listening also tends to earn you a chance to get it back.

Choose to be interested in what they say

You always have a choice on what you can be interested in. If the love of your partner is essential to you and you want to save your marriage, this is one of the things to add to your list. The problem can be that you tend to tune out whenever your spouse is talking; therefore, not even getting their point.

You do not get to choose the conversations you are interested in and the ones to ignore. You take the whole package. Pay attention to boring discussions as well as the interesting ones. It shows your spouse that if you are interested in what they have to say, then they are also interesting. Showing you are interested happens when you read that book or watch that movie that they recommended, do some activities that she likes, or caring about her friends. Doing some of these things will even give you ideas to talk about and therefore improve your conversations in general.

Write small notes for them

It is always the little things that keep the fire

burning. After having a conversation, you probably made a plan on how you are going to spend some time together. You can scribble down a note to tell her that you still remember the program, and you can't wait to see them.

An easy way to look at it is by scribbling down the information you send her on text messages. A simple note strategically placed that they will find out on their own is a creative way to make your partner smile. Writing the notes also shows that you went the extra mile to please them and is also a fun way to share your romance. The good thing about this is that your spouse can get the note when they are stressing, the note will help them ease out and know that they have somebody who cares about them and loves them. Always right the notes in a cheerful tone and leave an assurance of love.

Have regular, media free mealtimes

Having meals together is an essential avenue for communication. It is when you can enjoy each other's company while also enjoying a nice meal. However, nowadays, most meal times are ruined by social media and television. It happens because you are focusing on your phone or TV. Instead of the conversation, your spouse is trying to relay. To avoid this hitches, you should schedule for meal times that are social media free.

During such dinners, all you do is talk to your spouse. Talk about anything and everything that you want to tell them. It can act as a bonding moment for you two. You will be amazed by how therapeutic the time spent with your spouse is. If this works for you, you can even decide to change all meal times to media free. Once it becomes regular, it will be easier for both of you and is likely to improve your communication die to the regularity.

Make eye contact when talking

It shows that your body language is also in sync with the conversation. Eye contact with your spouse shows that you are listening and that you respect them. Include all other aspects of body language such as touch, nods, and smiles during conversations. Accompanying conversations with body language shows that you acknowledge the conversation going on, and you are in the moment.

Using the touch and eye contact effectively can come off as sexy to your partner, and therefore they will want to talk more with you. Giving your partner hints that you enjoy talking to them will encourage them to speak to you, and you are likely to get that reaction reciprocated.

Avoid single-word responses

When your partner asks you a question, you should answer it to the best of your ability. Answering open-ended questions with a yes or a no show that you are not attentive, and you want your partner to shut up. Thoughtful responses that answer the question will give your partner the guidance they need and show that you are a resourceful person that can help in solving your partner's problems.

Surface level responses should be avoidable at all costs, for they are not helpful and may even irk anger or disappointments in your spouse. Answer the issues that you can and inform them if you are not knowledgeable. It will save everyone's time, and you will be doing your part in helping where you can in the matter. Giving an in-depth answer shows your spouse that you are interested in communication, and you also care about them.

Designate a place for all your important reminders and dates

If it becomes a challenge to meet and plan your activities, you can allocate a place in your house where you write all your important issues. The areas can be a refrigerator door or a bulletin board, or anything you can improvise. The area chosen should have the sole purpose of posting valuable information. You can pass by the place to check if there is anything that your spouse wanted doing. The area offers a space that is exclusive to the two of you. You can also decide to be goofy around the place and remind each other of the love you share. That is a safe place and is a thing of your own. It is likely to boost communication between the two of you.

Add them on social media

Your spouse should be your best friend and the person most included in your life. Adding them on social media acts like you are inviting them to all parts of your life. Here they can see what you post, and you can also include them in your posts about things they like. Recommend them things you think they may find interesting and get to know the part of them that is active on social media. Send each other messages, like each other's pictures, and be your spouse's biggest fan. Doing all these things that best friends do is likely to turn you into best friends in the long run. Social media also provides another avenue for communication. Using it appropriately with your spouse is expected to improve your communication.

Chapter 9:

Ways to Build Personal Boundaries in a Marriage

Boundaries are what differentiate people from others. They define what a person can allow and what they cannot allow. They show the margin of habits that you can enable hence showing a sense of ownership. Having boundaries show that you are in control of your life and you, therefore, take responsibility for all that is happening in your life.

It gives you freedom since you can operate anywhere within the boundaries and not affect your partner. Boundaries help you keep the right people within you and keep the people that you cannot keep up with away from you. Everyone should have limits put in place since they define you. Explaining them to your partner also ensures that you are in agreement on both of your boundaries and can put up with each other's lifestyles.

Setting up boundaries is not an easy task, especially

for your partner to understand you. They allow you to know your place and how to act to be in harmony with your significant other. Some of the ways you can set your boundaries in marriage are as below.

How to deal with envy

Envy is a crucial issue when it comes to relationships. You may feel envious on how your partner acts around other people. A jealous partner sees themselves as powerless and not having options that can empower them. It causes you to be unhappy and overthink small actions, and this can cause problems in the relationship. Setting boundaries on interactions with other people are likely to reduce the situation where you feel envious of your partner. Agreeing on the extent of closeness that your partner can have with people will keep you less stressed since you know the extent that your significant other can go without worrying about any consequences that can come with it.

Learn how to evaluate situations

Different situations have different solutions. Learning how to analyze a situation before judging is essential since it gives your partner a chance to explain themselves so you can agree on whether it was within the boundary or not. It means that boundaries are just set guidelines for you to operate. Acting differently on different occasions should be analyzed before deciding whether it has gone against the limits you have set. You should, however, behave in ways that would benefit both of you in case a boundary may come in between the decision. Couples should also communicate on whether the matter in hand could be handled better given the set boundaries.

You are allowed to say no

When setting boundaries, it is essential to know that you can say no and are allowed to differ from your partner. Loving another person does not mean that you have to agree with everything that they have to say. Having a choice is an integral part of being an adult and being in love in general. Boundaries are limits which may involve conquering your fears, therefore, saying no has to be an option. The ability to say no also enables you to draw your boundaries and be honest with your partner, so they know what you like and what you do not.

Communicating your boundaries

The easiest way to make your boundaries known to your partner is by informing them. Setting boundaries in marriage and life, in general, is familiar to everyone. Still, for your significant other to know them and understand them deeply, you will need to explain your boundaries to them. Expressing your thoughts and feelings will enable your partner to know you better and conduct themselves in ways that you approve. Failure to communicate your boundaries will cause misunderstanding between you and your spouse, therefore, causing a rift that can obliterate the relationship. You should, therefore, find a way that you can explain your feelings and boundaries to your partner so that you can agree.

Understand the consequences of your behaviour

When you act nicely and loving towards people, you are likely to attract people that are loving and nice. When you act irresponsible and unloving, you will repel friendly people. When setting boundaries, partners should be allowed to make their own decisions and be responsible for them. You should also be aware of your habits and if they align with the boundaries you make. Your behaviour should be a reflection on what you expect from your significant other in terms of borders. Setting rules then going against them yourself will show that you are not responsible and that the boundaries are not relevant to you.

Be responsible to your spouse

You are both adults, and you should, therefore, be accountable to your spouse and not for your spouse. Everyone should individually be able to conduct their daily responsibility without dependability on the spouse. Your actions should show responsibility to your spouse, meaning you should consider their feelings when making your own decisions. Actions affecting your spouse's feelings negatively are not suitable for the relationship since they may cause disagreements. Everyone should have their own life without interference from their partner; this causes independence between the partners and makes boundaries more effective.

Respect between the partners

For boundaries to be effective, there should be

mutual respect between the partners. The best way to earn respect is by giving it yourself. The limitations set should be fair to everyone without implying that one partner is disrespectful to the other. The absolute limits should be comfortable for you and your spouse and should be reachable by agreeing with both of you. Also, once the boundaries are in place. Respecting your spouse is what will keep you from going past the set limits. For limits to be practical, you both have to be humble and be able to compromise so that the relationship can be healthy

Every marriage should have boundaries set that include both partners. The limits help to set the rules of the marriage so that you can both leave in peace with fewer arguments between each other. They also draw the line and give freedom on how you can act without going against what your partner believes. People are different and therefore setting your boundaries straight up with the person you love will make things easy for you in future since you will not have to go back and forth on things you have already agreed.

Chapter 10:

Showing Respect to your Spouse

Respect is the ultimate gesture that will build and grow your marriage for a lifetime. Therefore, here are tips on how to show your spouse that you love and respect them.

Listening to your partner

Paying attention to your partner shows that you care about them and that you enjoy talking to them. Through listening to your spouse, you get to learn new things about them and appreciate them. Giving your partner a chance to express themselves without judgment is a sign of respect. When you can spare your time to listen to their views and be able to accommodate them shows your spouse, they are worthy of your time and therefore makes them feel appreciated.

Speak positive things behind their back

You should always make your partner feel good about themselves. Speaking well of the significant other shows that you love them and you are their number one fan. It shows that you care, and this will give them the morale and zeal to go and conquer the day. When talking to your friends or anybody outside your marriage, you should always uplift your spouse. It also shows your friends that you are confident in the choice you made about your spouse since you see their potential and are therefore proud of them. Belittling your spouse paints a bad image for both you and your spouse; this is because it shows that you are weak at making choices. It also makes your spouse feel unappreciated and incapable, which may make them lose their drive in life; therefore even cause the marriage to fail.

Focus on what they do well

Nobody is perfect. Accepting this statement will make your marriage life more comfortable since you will be able to see past your significant other's mistakes and appreciate their strong points. Seeing past their mistakes and being able to forgive is vital to maintain a healthy relationship. You should, however, focus on what they are good at since that is what matters the most. Your attitude towards your partner should always show you how much of a fantastic person they are. Every time it happens, you should remind them and use them to cheer them up. Keeping the right moments in mind will help you counter the bad moments that come since you will always have something to look up to and assure yourself that you married the right person. If they do something good for you, you should always show gratitude. It shows that you appreciate the act and will make them do more actions of the same sort.

Encourage them

Your significant other may be going through challenges that may be family-related or different. When they share the difficulties they are facing, you should encourage them and assist them where necessary. Help can come in various ways, such as a listening ear, an action to be taken, or advice needed. Notice the type of support you can offer in the situation provided by your partner and do your best to help them accomplish their wishes. Notice their efforts if they make progress on the issue and affirm them to ensure them that they added moving in the right direction. Struggling is standard among everybody; however, having somebody by your side through every step of the struggle shows that they care about you and respect you.

Find ways to solve conflicts

Arguments are bound to arise when you are in a relationship. However, these are just challenges that any strong relationship should be able to endure and get through. Finding the right ways to solve your arguments is a skill you should all acquire since there will be many times you will need to use the expertise. If your spouse does something that irritates you in front of a crowd, you should find a way to correct them. Preferable means to solve arguments are when you are alone and can, therefore, discuss the matter in detail. The choice of words used during a marriage is also essential. The words should show respect and not affect your partner's feelings even after the argument is over. How you solve your issues shows how much you respect your partner since words said when angry could have a more damaging effect than intended. Arguing in front of other people shows that you lack respect for each other.

Think before you speak

People are different. Understanding how your partner communicates is essential so that you can also align your communication so that you can understand each other easily. Life can have its intimidating moments. Choosing your words will influence how your partner makes their decisions when faced with such problems. Men and women reason differently. Understanding your spouse's way of thinking, and their choice of words will make it easier to encourage them. Understanding their thought process also helps you to know how to package sensitive information when presenting it to them without offending them. Making snap judgments and sneaky comments may come off as disrespectful to your significant other.

Constant reminders of love

Staying with somebody for a long time may lead you to start taking them for granted. Constant reminders of love rekindle the fire between the two of you. It is vital to assure your partner that they were your choice, and they are still your choice to date. It is crucial that both of you in the relationship feel loved and are sure that they are the first option to the other. Affection can be shown directly or indirectly, through words or actions. Understanding

your partner's love language makes it easier to
express your love for them in ways that they will
appreciate and know that they are loved and
respected in the relationship.

Avoid comparisons

Comparison is the thief of joy. Comparing your
partner to someone will come off as belittling or
that you do not appreciate them enough. It shows
that you would rather be with the other person than
with them. Comparisons should only come up when
talking about strengths or achievements. Comparing
their successes to their role models will show the
progress and shows that you notice the change. It is
also likely to encourage them to work harder since
you believe in them, and they would not want to let
you down. Unfavourable comparisons show that you
lack respect for your partner and will ruin the
marriage.

Chapter 11:

Getting your Spouse to Open Up

Does your husband or wife seem to withdraw from you and keep to themselves? This is a sign of something troubling their minds. Such situations could lead to depression. This is why it's vital to try and help your spouse open up and talk about their troubles or worries. Here are some tips on achieving that.

Do not text

Texting inhibits sharing a lot of information. We send texts when sharing quick and light hearted communication. You should never discuss important issues via text. You should, therefore, avoid interaction with your spouse on important matters on text message. Discussing serious issues should be face to face.

Discussing matters face to face allows seriousness and control of the conversation. It is because you will be able to study your partner's body language and gauge the direction of the conversation. Face to face conversations give you a chance to read emotion and even listen to the tone of your partner's voice, which is not available when you use texting.

If it becomes impossible to have face to face conversations, you should at least conduct the communications via a phone call or a video call—use text messages when you are talking about irrelevant information such as sports or movies.

Talk about your own experiences

You can't be sure about what your partner is feeling. All you can do is make assumptions. Making assumptions about your partner will make them act defensively. It can hinder effective communication since they will be focusing on defending themselves instead of addressing the problems you are facing. You should, therefore, talk about yourself and how you are feeling.

Since you understand yourself the most, it will be easier to explain your thoughts, actions and feelings. Taking about yourself shows that you take responsibility for your actions and therefore allow your spouse to explain themselves and give justification for their efforts. Talking about yourself makes you be the vulnerable one. Seeing this, your partner is not likely to get defensive, and they are likely also to take the opportunity to be vulnerable and open up to you.

The extent you explain yourself also tells your spouse how they should explain themselves and the extent of information they should give. Using this trick to your advantage will have your partner easily opening up about anything you feel like talking about.

Ask for what you are willing to give

You should always be willing to take the lead in the relationship. From this, your partner is likely to follow in your footsteps. And you can both have an easy time in the marriage. By taking the lead, it will be easy for you to initiate the change you want in your relationship. Immediately you notice a problem; you should be the one to find a way to bring it up for discussion.

Waiting on your partner to initiate these conversations can cause a lot of stress since it will come off as playing games, and nobody likes playing

guessing games. Owning up and conducting the
conversations will give you control of how you want
the direction and flow of the conversation to go.
Make a plan of how, when and where you plan on
having the conversation beforehand. Having these
plans makes it easy for your partner to come and
participate in the conversation.

Your spouse may be stubborn and trying to avoid
having the conversation. In this case, you also need
to be stubborn and keep scheduling for the talk
until you are successful. If both of you become
reluctant, it will cause the conversation to postpone
or even never to happen. When reaching out, you
should be very vague to keep them curious about the
talk.

Make it painless

Nobody likes experiencing pain, and nobody will
intentionally put themselves in a situation that will
cause them discomfort. Therefore, when intending
to talk with your partner, you need to clarify to
them that it will be a discussion and not an
interrogation. When the conversation feels like
grilling, it is likely to make your spouse
uncomfortable, and they may be dodgy to

participate. Making it friendly and owning up to your mistakes makes it more familiar and easy to handle.

When alone with your spouse, you can decide to be vulnerable; this shows then that you trust them and that they can also become susceptible around you. Sharing about your thoughts and emotions will give them a chance also to share their feelings. When both of you contribute to the conversation, it makes it easier for both of you, and the conversation becomes enjoyable.

Do not concern yourself with your partner's intentions

When getting into the discussion, both of you can have different expectations from the discussion. However, when preparing for this, you should only be concerned about your intentions. After all, you can never know precisely your partner's intentions.

All you can do is make assumptions which can either be true or false. Instead of making assumptions, save yourself the hassle and wait to hear what your partner has to say. Keeping only your intentions in mind will give you the chance to focus on yourself. From this, you can explain how you feel in detail and make sure your partner understands what you have to say. Doing this will make you look sincere and honest and therefore encourage your partner to do the same.

In some cases, both the intentions of you and your spouse may be the same. It does not matter, but if that happens, then it will have worked in your favour because your partner will see that you mean well and that you are on the same team.

Be patient

Opening up is not an easy thing to do. You should be patient with your spouse and give them space when it looks like things are getting out of hand. Failure to open up is a habit that you noticed on your partner Breaking a habit is very hard and may not be achievable after having one conversation.

Breaking entrenched patterns is not easy; however, once you start the journey, you can be sure to deal with the problem and eradicate it in the long run. You can also track the progress and see how you are performing. Always show appreciation to your partner and express that you look forward to future conversations.

It shows your significant other that you enjoy communicating with them and that you are aware of the progress they are making. It encourages them and makes them look forward to future conversations with you and continue with the process in the future.

Chapter 12:

Things you should Discuss with your Spouse – Often

As you'll see in the next chapter, there's nothing as complex as initiating a heavy subject of discussion to your spouse. Depending on how the two of you relate, and the nature of the topic, the scale might go up on the complex side. Either way, that doesn't mean that you should brush off burning matters. In this chapter, you'll visit ten commonly assumed topics that married couples should discuss in detail and as often as required.

1. *The Sex Talk*

Now, this is hands down the most complex topic of all. No one wants to be told they are bad in bed, or that they don't satisfy you as a spouse should. However, on the same note, no one wants to keep having sex with someone who gets them only halfway there. Therefore, discussing your sexual desires with your spouse will benefit both of you. If you'd like more foreplay before the 'did' begins, then let your spouse know. How would you like it done, and where do you like to be kissed or touch. Speaking of disappointments, nothing bruises a man's ego like telling them that they aren't man enough to satisfy their own wife. Therefore, as you hold this discussion, don't go all negative on their performance. Be respectful to him – or even her – throughout.

Start the conversation by telling them what you like about their sex. Bring memories of the best moments you had during, before or after sex and let them know that you'd like more of that. In fact, this is the one conversation you're allowed to get sexual while discussing. Touch them as you talk, give them pecks and what not. Ask them what they think about your performance. Listen, you know you're about to throw some solid shade (politely) on them, so whatever they tell you won't hurt that much. So bait yourself. Let them open up, promise to do more of what they like, then give them a few requests on what you like.

See the worst thing about not discussing your sexual desires is, you'll end up very frustrated and this might easily lead to infidelity. All it'll take is a third

party telling you the crazy things they can do to you,
and you cave. We're all human, we want to feel
loved and spoiled. So tell your spouse how to
achieve just that.

After this talk, guide them during the next session.
Don't direct them like freaking George Clooney; no
just lead their hand, whisper a slight instruction to
their ears, when they do something you like, tell
them to keep going. Within no time, they'll
understand your body and desires, and will make
love to you till your brains fall out.

2. His Friends and Family

Yes, these should be the most important parties in
his life. However, let's face it, not all friends and
families are good. Some are ill-willed with jealousy
and malice. These are the people you should talk to
your spouse about. You're not gossiping or trying to
make your spouse hate them; you are just airing
your thoughts about them. Therefore, keep the
approach polite and 100% respectful. Remember
they were in his or her life before you came along.
Even if they came after you, they still hold a big
spot. So when should you approach your spouse
about their friends and family?

- When they plan to destroy your marriage

- When they call to insult you or threaten you
- When they make moves that can drive your spouse to infidelity
- When they are rude to you during gatherings

Just because you are married to them, doesn't mean you have to put up with the madness coming from their friends and family. Hence, approach him or her about them. Take note, if you don't make an effort to get along with these people, it won't mean a dime when complaining to your spouse about them. In fact, you'll appear as the bad guy. So make a genuine effort to talk to them, and get along. If this doesn't seem to work, then talk to your spouse. Go with some facts and evidence to show your spouse that you're not just accusing his people falsely. Respect these people during the conversation and don't insult them to your spouse. Use very general terms to describe their attitude towards you. Again, brushing off such things will hurt your marriage in the long run.

3. *Your Career and Goals*

When single, or just dating, you were in a position to do as you please and work all day and night if that's what a job required from you. Sadly, once married, you may need to cut off some working hours to attend to this new family. Unfortunately, sometimes you may get so busy and end up forgetting about your future plans and dreams. Those career goals you had before marriage should still stand after marriage, until you achieve them. Talk to your partner if you feel like you're lagging behind with your career. Such personal issues can make you withdraw from the relationship, or even recent your spouse for the things you weren't able to achieve. This is quite normal, that's why discussing the situation with your spouse helps both of you know what's happening and how to sort it in both your interests.

In case your spouse had career goals, and he seems not motivated about them anymore, also approach them, and find out what killed the motivation. Be their motivation and allow them to be yours. A perfect marriage is one where both partners are achieving their dreams. So don't set your dreams aside for marriage, they will catch up and either make you miserable or end the marriage to pursue them.

4. *Your Finances*

JEAN-CLAUDE
LEVEQUE

Okay. Keep it real; does your spouse spend more than they should, or are they so stingy they can't allow you to get new underwear till the old ones wear out? This is a serious issue to be discussed on occasion. In fact, if you could run a monthly discussion on monthly expenditure, that would not only build your relationship but your financial situation as well. Having monthly discussions will help each new month start on a positive note, and all your financial plans will be met without much struggle.

When the house needs something, discuss it. Assuming that things are obvious and that your spouse should know about them, is the biggest mistake you can make. Just because you earn more than your spouse doesn't make you "the boss". Marriage should be a 50-50 situation making everyone feel valued and respected. Listen to each other's opinions and plans, and blend in to ensure you're at par.

Your Past and its Current Effects

Sometimes your past events catch up with you. The fear and trauma surfaces and you withdraw from your marriage. Don't. Have a chat with your spouse and tell them about such occurrences. If you lost someone and had a dream about them, and suddenly the grief comes back, sit down with your spouse and cry your feelings out. Let them see you when vulnerable; this will help them understand you more and help you trust them with such issues.

If the situation is so bad it requires professional help, don't leave your spouse behind. This is not a journey you want to travel alone. You need a support system, and your spouse needs to feel trusted and relied on. Take them with you and let them stand by you as you heal from the past. Whether the past occurrence was your fault or not, it's important to be open and honest about it. This is the only way to get rid of it for good.

Your Frequent Arguments

Discuss your discussions. Why do they always end up in fights? Is it possible to come up with a formula for discussing issues of concern? Can you create a safe word for when the discussion escalates into an argument so you can both take a timeout? If you argue about every single thing, then it means your personalities differ in lengths, and that's a reason for divorce. So before it gets to that, talk about it.

During this discussion, both of you should list down the things you fight most about. You'd be surprised that it's the same thing over and over. So what's the real issue? Try and get to the bottom of each argument. For example; you've argued about the toilet seat every day in the last week. The argument escalates so much that you can't face each other or one of you cries.

Considering the nature of the situation, a toilet seat is not a big deal. At least not big enough to cause friction. However, maybe during minor confrontations, one of you brings up past issues. Now that could turn a discussion into an argument. The other issue would be if, during a confrontation, one of you goes off the handle and unnecessarily overreacts.

So, once you've identified the cause of all arguments during simple discussions, you can come up with a valid solution for it.

More things to discuss is health problems, work stress, fears and worries, and such issues. This will help you strengthen your bond as a couple and make your marriage last. Keep in mind to approach the discussion with politeness, patience, understanding and respect.

Chapter 13:

How to Initiate "The Talk"

During your marriage, you or your spouse might request to have "The Talk". This is the talk that can either build your love or destroy everything you've worked on thus far. This makes your approach on "The Talk" very crucial and in dire need of a good strategy. So, how can you initiate "The Talk" and ensure it flows smoothly and ends successfully saving your marriage? Here are a few tips.

Define your Expectations
How do you want the conversation to conclude? Sometimes complex conversations end well, and most time – depending on your approach – may end on a negative note. This thought might scare you off and make you shy from the conversation or start the conversation on a negative note. Stay positive-minded; before and during the conversation.

What's your agenda for initiating this talk?

Don't go into a conversation without knowing what kind of information or closure you're trying to achieve from it. If you're looking for answers, then know what answer will satisfy your curiosity. If you want to give your spouse some answers or explanations, then know the details and how to deliver. The worst part of having a conversation is thinking about it two days later and going, "Damn I should have said or asked this." But now it's too late to revisit the chapter. Knowing what you want out of a conversation will help you prolong it until you've quenched your thirst.

Accept the Nature of the Conversation

Go into the conversation knowing that it's a hard one, and it might trigger different emotions from you and your spouse. Be ready for anything, but hold yourself together when the worst comes.

Just Start Talking

Dilly dallying doesn't help the conversation go smooth. Most complex conversations will hold pretty strong emotions and reactions, so just start talking. Read the room, read your spouse's mood and start with a direct question or statement. Don't hint that you want to discuss something. In case they have or get a clue, they may look for a way to escape that conversation.

Think about that Starting Sentence

Don't just start talking. As you read the room, analyze the temperature and know the best way to start the sentence. Think about the tone you're about to use on your spouse and how it'll affect the conversation. Prep that statement or question; are there any offensive words? Does it seem more like an accusation than an inquiry? Is it a question that'll make them - or you – comfortable to address, or immediately cave?

Avoid Manipulating your Spouse

You've probably thought about this talk for a while now, maybe even for weeks; therefore, remember it'll be a total ambush to your spouse. The environment in which you initiate this conversation matters. Inviting your spouse to a casual and fun public place just to bombard them with questions is total manipulation. Even discussing your marital issues in public – whether or not others can hear you – is wrong and unfair. Make sure the environment is comfortable for each of you to talk and express yourselves.

Choose the Right Time

No! Talking before, during, or right after having sex with your spouse is the absolute wrong time to discuss heavy issues. When your mind is aroused, you are only after sex, and your judgment is clouded. Your spouse will tell you what you want to hear just to end the conversation faster and get to bed. On the other hand, you'll agree to shoddy explanations just to get to the activity that both of you seem to agree on. If your spouse tries to get touchy or sexual with you during the conversation, read the red flag and immediately know he's escaping the conversation.

Also, don't wake your spouse in the middle of the night and start "The Talk." Be patient and wait for the right time. When they seem to be in a relaxed mood. Also, check your mood. If the talk is about something your spouse did and your mood is on the scale of eating them alive, hang in there. Don't approach them in such a time, because the conversation won't go well and the chances are, you won't get the answers you need. Worst of all, they might walk out on you or even suggest a split from you. Initiate the talk when you are calm, and all the anger has left your system. Remember anger clouds judgment as well.

Don't Set a Trap

As bad as this may sound, your talk should be done at a place where your spouse can freely walk out on you. Yes! Walk out. No one should be forced into a conversation or cornered to do something they are not comfortable with. So, don't start the talk while flying or driving. Most people opt for these places so that the spouse doesn't have an option but to respond to them. Here's some advice; the best conversation is when you both want to discuss the issue, and such conversations end with a better marital bond.

Plan "The Talk"

While guilty spouses may try to run from a conversation, hence why sometimes it's not advisable to give them a heads-up, it's good to tell your spouse that you have a burning issue and plan on when and where to discuss it. To be on the safe side, show them that the issue doesn't bother you that much and that it won't change your marital status. This way, they'll be eager and comfortable to talk to you because you appear reasonable.

Have Facts and Evidence if Possible

When about to accuse someone of something, it's

important to have either evidence or facts. If you want to tell your spouse to ease off on being rude to you, then ensure you can clearly explain the different scenarios when he was rude with you. This isn't to say that you open a folder of mistakes in your mind and pile up files then throw at them in the future. Approaching each situation after it has happened is the best way to solve it. Why? Because it's fresh in your mind and your spouse's mind as well. If it's something you found out about, then ensure you have evidence. If not, then either wait till you can gather evidence, or approach them with a question. Without facts, you'll never know when or if your spouse is pretending or lying; and you can't really base an argument on instincts alone.

Respect your Spouse as you Talk
Even if your spouse is on the wrong, don't look down on them. Shouting, insulting or throwing rude words at them won't help the conversation or your marriage. As they explain their point of view, even if you strongly disagree, remain silent and listen to them. After which, politely correct them or give them your opinion. Never make them sound stupid or clueless. Guide the conversation in an intelligent and mature manner. Such moves help the other party realize their mistake faster.

Conclude in Unison

As you end the talk, ensure you're both satisfied with the outcome. Make a conclusion or agreement that works for both of you. Don't suggest and assume that your spouse is okay with it. Ask them for their opinion and suggestions, weigh all options together and conclude in unison.

Know when to Involve a Third Party

Not all complex conversations end with an agreement. Sometimes the Pandora's Box opens, and the situation becomes more complex than initially anticipated. In such a case, agree to request further assistance from a professional. In case you have a mutual friend with whom you trust and have always relied on through all your marital issues, give them a call, set a date and revisit the talk in their presence. This friend has to be very neutral and trustworthy (without bad intentions). In case either of you doubts the friend, then go for a therapist.

Bonus tip:

Never start a complex conversation when your spouse seems moody or stressed about a related or non-related situation. They won't have the time or energy to spare.

Chapter 14:

Timeout from your Partner

Taking time off in a marriage sounds like a scary move that could eventually lead to a divorce. Well not necessarily. Sometimes it's the one thing a marriage requires to keep going. Time away from each other will clear your thoughts and provide enough space to think through everything. A relationship can sometimes clog your mind with the thousands of situations happening all at once. During this time, you're bound to make decisions and moves that will permanently damage your union. Thus, going away will help you rethink and make thoughtful decisions.

Before you decide to take a break from your spouse, there are a few things to know and do.

Talk about the Break with your Spouse
Sometimes the decision to take a break is made in

the midst of an argument. Even so, it's important to discuss the break again with your spouse. If you just had an argument, you'd rather sleep on separate beds and when morning comes, you meet for a conversation. Never make decisions when angry or during a fight.

When discussing taking a break, talk about the reasons behind it. Make your spouse understand why you feel a break is important and the depth of the situation. Not every tiny misunderstanding deserves a break. You might be surprised that this discussion can solve so many issues that you'll no longer require time off. When a spouse has reached a point whereby they are requesting a break, it shows the partner that if things aren't resolved as should, then a break up will occur. Therefore, most times, the "let's take a break" conversation, ends up solving the issues at hand. This is because people don't make corrections or one's cries seriously until they realize that they are about to lose them.

Agree on a Specific Time Frame
Taking a break means getting away to gather your energy after feeling drained in the marriage. Therefore, it all depends on how much you feel drained to set a time frame for your recovery. It's more like rehab for your mind. If you're the one

suggesting taking a break, then suggest the timeframe. If your spouse needs a break, then allow him to set the timeframe. Once a timeframe is requested, discuss it and come to an agreement.

A reasonable time frame is like a week or 3. If your spouse requests for five months, he or she is breaking up with you. If they ask for a month timeframe, you can try and negotiate. A longer timeframe will give you or your spouse a chance to enjoy single life and rethink marriage, and that's not right.

Set Some Break Rules
As you discuss taking a break, lay down some break rules. The dos and don'ts during this period should be set straight to avoid issues in the future. Keep in mind that a break from a boyfriend is not similar to one from a husband or wife. Therefore, things like dating other people during the break is not appropriate. Here are a few rules to set;

- No Communication – If you keep texting and calling each other then there's no need for a break. Your mind will remain clogged and your judgment clouded. To keep it healthy, you can agree on one text a week of one correspondence, where you tell each other that you're fine and healthy. That's it.

- No meet ups – Just like talking, meeting your spouse during this time off won't help the situation. In fact, agree to not see each other at all during this period. If possible, go to a different city, state or country to be as far away from them as possible.

- No dating – no matter the magnitude of conflict between you and your spouse, deciding to date other people might bring about feelings of jealousy and insecurity; and as mentioned, it will give each party a reason to split.

- Sharing items – Agree on how you'll take care of pets during the break. Who'll go with what and who'll remain with the rest. This does not include house furniture.

- Avoid family and friends – while they can be good comfort, such people may influence your decisions depending on their personal opinions and that might hurt your marriage. Agree to avoid discussing the issue with anyone during the break. Therefore, all aspects of your decisions will be only based on your minds and hearts and not outside influence.

Change Environment

One relaxing aspect of a break is the change of environment. Step out of your comfort zone; in fact it'd be better if you visited a new city. Make it a solo vacation. Relax your mind and explore the area. For the first few days, your mind shouldn't even think about your marriage situation. This way the anger leaves you and all negative emotions don't worry you anymore. If you're financially capable, the make different trips to different places. However, make time to sit and think. Communicate with your feelings, dig deep and get to know what you really want from this marriage.

Accept Faults and Come Up with Solutions

This is the time to accept your partaking in the marital misunderstandings. Where did you go wrong, and what are your faults? It's not always about blaming your spouse. Digging into your own weaknesses will help you know how to go about communication when you get back home. Try and identify everything that makes your relationship go wrong. Ask yourself what you can work on and be honest with your feelings.

Going Back Home

After the freeing trip, go back to your spouse with a positive attitude. Be excited to see them, and start by telling them about the experiences you had – if any. Forget the problems you had before for a minute. Listen to their experiences as well laugh about a hundred things then get to the story.

There's no rule to when you should discuss pending matters. So, you can spend a few days with your spouse before addressing the matter. When it's time to have the talk, be silent and listen to your spouse. Understand how much growth they've had during the break.

4 Signs you need to take a Break from Your Marriage

There are different kinds of fallouts in a marriage. Some issues can be solved with one talk, while others require professional assistance. All this is reliant on the magnitude of the fallout. However, it's not advisable to take a break when your spouse sneezes. Requesting a break every single time, shows your spouse that you're ready to leave the marriage over minor issues. It also shows that you're not willing to fight for your love, or maybe you're just not in love with your spouse.

Therefore, when do you know it's time to take a

break, but not really break up? Here are 4 signs.

Every Conversation Turns into an Argument

Does your marriage seem like a funny story turned sour without warning? No matter how much you try to live a day without arguing with your spouse, it's all in vain. It has come to the point whereby arguing feels like a norm, and that it gets awkward if you don't argue. Don't get used to misunderstandings; those are signs that your marriage is failing.

These situations normally occur when one or both partners are falling out of love. They may also occur when a spouse is stressed or depressed about work, family, friends, finances, health, and the like. In this case, their stress or anger is misplaced and directed at you. Giving your spouse some space will help them separate the issues and realize who they are truly angry with. Giving them time will help them sort those problems and regain positive energy towards you.

If the arguments occur due to you and your spouse growing apart, taking a break will help both of you recollect and have ample time to decide whether or not you want to continue with the marriage.

Everything Else seems more important than the Relationship

When your work or separate personal lives seem more important than the relationship, then it's time to take a break. Your spouse should always be your number one fan and your priority. Yes, everything else around you is essential, and you can't live without; but those things shouldn't be the reason to creating a wall in your marriage.

In such cases, you'd find yourselves not having time to even talk about how the day was. You live like two strangers on one house. Your life becomes a routine where you wake up, shower, have silent or separate breakfasts, leave for work, come back and have silent or separate dinners, shower then sleep in your corner facing the wall.

It's not that you hate each other or are tired of each other, it's that all your energy is focused on the wrong thing. Taking a break will help you re-energize and re-organize yourself enough to spare some time and energy for every aspect of your life, favouring your marriage more.

If both of you ended up focused more on other things, then a talk would probably solve the issue; however, if it's one spouse, then a break is crucial for them to gather their thoughts.

Your Marriage isn't Growing
Before you got married, you and your spouse had all

these dreams and goals for when you get married. However, here you are and nothing seems to have been achieved. Did the flame blow out after the honeymoon? Something must have happened to prevent you from either pursuing or achieving your marriage goals.

Time off and away from each other will help you think through those dreams and at what point in your marriage, they became invalid. This will help you spot the loopholes in your marriage, and figure out how to get back to building your marriage emotionally and financially.

There are Signs of Infidelity

Infidelity is wrong and should be unforgivable; but it would be unfair to both you and your spouse to end your marriage due to cheating. While a cheater's always a cheater, there are other factors that lead a faithful man into cheating. The biggest mistake people make is to blame the partner who cheated for wrecking their marriage. That's entirely not on them.

Maybe they came to you with a problem but you were too busy to listen, so they found solace in someone else's arm or bed. No one is justifying cheating, but no one is a saint, so these things are bound to happen in certain scenarios.

Anyway, after an infidelity occurrence, you both deserve timeout to see if you can spot the issues that led to infidelity. Are these issues solvable? Are you willing to accept your contribution to the infidelity? Most importantly, are you willing to forgive your spouse for cheating?

If you find out that your spouse cheated once, you may decide to forgive him or her (this entirely depends on you). Unfortunately, if you realize that your spouse had been cheating long before you walked down the aisle, then honey, there's really nothing to save there. Either way, taking a break helps you gather your thoughts, appreciate yourself, and prevent yourself from falling into depression. The best decisions are made when calm.

If you're looking to win a minor fight, that's not a reason to take a break. Couples don't take breaks to prove a point. They take breaks to gather thoughts and control their mental state. They also take breaks when their hearts want to stay in the marriage but actually fix things and be happy. Taking thousands of breaks will make your marriage lose meaning and your spouse lose interest in you entirely.

It's unfortunate that most breaks end in divorces; that said, try your best to solve all your issues with a conversation. If you need a break, sleep in a different room, or take a casual vacation. During a break some spouses opt to let go and use their energy on something else. That time apart might make them miss being single and want that life back. Only take breaks when you've tried a conversation and therapy, and they both don't seem to work.

Five things to ask yourself before taking a break

Will it lead to a break-up?

Many people believe that taking a break is just among the first steps leading to a break-up. While this might sometimes be the case, there are exceptions where breaks can be helpful and redeem a marriage. However, because most people use the excuse a break just before asking for a break up from their spouse has led to a negative perception breaks.

However, as we all know, breaks are not as bad as many people may think or portray. You can use breaks as an excuse before a break up thinking it is an excellent idea to let your spouse go slowly. You expect that it will be easier to let go once they have been on the break and seen that they can survive on their own without the relationship. In reality, you are just a coward who is scared to speak their mind. You intend to use this tactic to shield yourself from the guilt that will haunt you once you inform your spouse that you need to divorce. You should, therefore, be honest with yourself and be sure whether you want to break up or you need a break.

If you think there is no way the marriage is going to work, you need to inform your spouse immediately and save them the torture. Offering a break is likely to extend their suffering. Since all through the break, they will be thinking about all the uncertainties available. Using a break instead of breaking is just postponing a problem.

Therefore, before suggesting for a break, you need to be sure whether you want a break or it will eventually lead to divorce. Having your mind set up and having the courage to explain your choice to your spouse will save time and cause less pain so you can g back to being happy eventually.

Why are you taking a break?

Being honest with yourself will make things easier for you and your spouse in making decisions. Find the real reason why you want to take the break and avoid any cover-up reasons that you may want to use not to seem petty or needy. Being honest with yourself and your spouse is the first step to see whether the relationship can be saved it not. Sit down with your partner and discuss the issues you are facing.

Try to discuss with them to see whether the issues can be resolvable or not. If it is behaviours that your partner has, you can talk to them and see whether they are willing to change or not. The clearer you explain what is bugging you to your partner, the more likely they are to understand your point, and you may stand a chance in salvaging your relationship. If you want to take a break to prove a point to your spouse, make sure that you have explained to them your reasons clearly.

Failure to explain to them the clear reasons will lead to mental torture which nobody deserves. You also need to ask yourself if the timing is right. Why are you choosing this moment for the break? Is it a good time? Will it affect any upcoming activities that you had planned? Having your reasons right before deciding on the break up is essential. If there are changes that you think might be the reason for the break you should talk to your spouse to see if there is anything you can do about it.

Breaks are serious matters and should not be decided on after a heated argument or a small disagreement. You need to sit down, relax and assess all available options before settling on the break option.

Are you willing to lose them?

Breaks are very risky since they reveal a lot to you. Being in a relationship blinds a lot of things from you since you only concentrate on your spouse and yourself or kids if you have any. When you go on a break with your significant other, they may not want to come back after the break, even if they were the ones who were against the break, to begin with. Breaks come with no guarantees.

Spending time away from each other can show you that you are better off alone than with your spouse. It will, therefore, be challenging to come back to the relationship if you know that you will be more comfortable when you live on your own that when you are with them. However, the same can happen to your partner, where they notice that they do not need you at all. It can come as a surprise and leave you stranded and heartbroken. Therefore before deciding on taking a break, you need to know the

JEAN-CLAUDE
LEVEQUE

risks that come with it. Try any possible solution to stay together. Weigh your options to see whether the break is worth it.

What are the ground rules and how long will it work.

Taking a break is going to need your own customized rules that you should set, and both of you should agree on before agreeing to go on the break. Sit down with your spouse and decide on the rules together. It is so that the rules do not seem unfair to anyone. Talk about whether you are allowed to see other people or not. You chose someone you are attracted to, so you need to settle for the idea that someone else may also find them attractive. Decide on whether you are allowed to see other people, and if it happens, how you will deal with it once the break is over. You also to decide on how long the break will go on for.

Some people may leave it open-ended while others can set a date where you will come together and analyze the situation to see if there are any changes. Whichever answer you pick, always make sure you discussed it with your significant other, so they do not stay in limbo with half-baked information. The rules made should be adhered to by both of you.

Consequences should also be set together so that you know how to go about when the rules are broken.

Do you want to have contact?

Before going on the break, you need to decide whether you will still want to communicate with your spouse or not. Check the technicalities and determine whether it will be right for you to keep contact or cut them off completely during this period. Some people think that staying in touch will cloud your judgment and you be free as you want to. Lacking contact to them means that you can see the world differently and get new perspectives that you could not know when you were in the relationship.

However, everybody has their perspective on the dos and don'ts of a break. Since it is your choice to go on the break, you make all the rules that come with it. Decide with the guidance of your spouse on the rules that will favour both of you. So you can both have an easy time while on the break.

Benefits of Taking Breaks

Getting some space

Breaks help provide you with the space that you both need. When you spend a lot of time with somebody, it can get tiresome, especially if you have been married for a while and are living together. It may seem that there is always something coming up that is making you argue every time. These issues can create a permanent rift between the two of you if it is not taken care of immediately. Wanting some space is right for you mentally. It enables you to clear your mind, and you can examine everything at your comfort.

You know you need space when you start having mixed feelings about your partner. It can come as a result of your assumptions, or something that your partner does that irritates you. Taking a break will give you the space you need away from your partner, where you can examine your relationship and the direction it is taking. Space also gives you a taste of what life will look like without your partner. From your analysis of both worlds, You will decide whether you are happier when with or without your spouse. It gives you a clear perspective so you can make the next decision with a rational mind.

Finding yourself

Being in a relationship can be very consuming, and you may tend to lose yourself due to all the responsibility that comes with it. It is because your spouse's life may get too much in your way that you forget all about the life you had before. Even when in a relationship, you need to be independent on your own. And not entirely depending on your partner. It can be almost impossible to balance your life, and that is why many people get sucked in and lose themselves. A break can come in handy once you notice such tendencies happening in your marriage. You need a break where you can reconnect to the person you were before you fell in love with your partner.

Remember the old days when you were fun and full of ambition, remember all the things you promised yourself you would do before hitting a certain age. Life got in the way, and you ended up in an eternal circle of routine. But this is now your chance to have your life back. Take that class you always wanted or visit that place you ever wanted to but could not because of the relationship pressure.

Link up with old friends and catch up and see what they have made of their lives while you were busy with yours. From this, you can get a new perspective on life and learn a thing or two that can benefit you now or in the future. Remind yourself of who you were while you have fun. Doing this is essential for your relationship since you get to experience things on your own, and you can come and teach your partner something new. Remember, you are responsible for your happiness and not anybody else.

Figure out your priorities in life and life goals

A break gives you some time to think. Use this time to analyze your life and what you have attained so far. See how your priorities have changed over time. From the time you started the relationship to now when you are taking a break. Life has flown by. Luckily here is your chance to go back to the drawing board. Better late than never. Look at the life goals that you have attained, the ones you threw away, and the new ones you have set. Also, check your spouse's priorities and goals.

After spending all that time together, you should know exactly how they live and what they intend to get out of life. Check to see if your priorities and goals align. If your goals are aligned, you can go and mend things with your partner as you decide on how you can help each other achieve both of your goals. Working as a team will make the goals easily achievable than working alone. However, if your priorities and goals collide, you can decide on whether to mend things and seek help or do away with the relationship if it is not salvageable. Time apart will show you what is most important to you; focus on it to achieve your goals.

Learn if you are compatible

Finding two fully compatible people is very rare. Most couples are very different, but you tend to learn how to leave with each other. There are usually several differences between you and your partner. Acknowledging them and deciding to work on them is what determines whether you are compatible or not. When taking the break, you need to check how compatible you are with your partner. It is a sensitive matter that may need a lot of focus when doing.

However, the break provides you with ample time and space to do this task. Think about all the things you have in common, the things you agree on, and the ones you disagree with. Check whether you still like them, and you are still sexually attracted to them. Answering these questions will give you a clear picture of whether you two are compatible or not. Based on the outcome you get, you can then decide on your next decision after thorough research.

Is it love or friendship?

You ended up with your spouse because you were in love, and that is why you got married. However, things change, and so do people. The person you once loved can now be a different person whom you can be friends; on the other hand; you could now even be more in love with them. To make a decision, a break is crucial. You can be genuinely in love with your spouse, but there is something that seems off. Take the break to have a proper analysis of what is going on. A break will help you to understand whether you still love your partner or if you are better off as friends.

Are you still sexually attracted to your partner? If not, then you are probably better off as friends. It is just among the many questions you can ask to check whether you still have feelings for them. Include

other items that can have what your description of
what you feel is love and what you think is
friendship is. From the answers, you get you will
have a well-thought answer of whether it is love or
friendship, and you can now make a decision you
will favour you the most.

Miss each other

Being around each other all the time can make you
take your partner for granted most of the time.
Spending some time apart will make you appreciate
each other and remember why you chose them over
anyone else in the first place. You give yourself a
chance to miss each other and know the impact that
your spouse has on you. Noticing their absence is
right for you since it will help you to understand
how important your partner is to you and whether
or not you can live without them. However,
spending time apart may show you that you do not
miss your partner at all. It can be a sad realization
that the person you once loved does not mean a
thing to you anymore. It is unfortunate, but you will
now have to decide on whether you will work on it
or let it go.

Rekindle spark

Breaks sometimes are the most useful ways to show you just how much a person means to you. Time and distance can be an excellent trigger to know that you miss your partner, and you need them back in your life. Your relationship can be facing a hard time where you lack intimacy, or the spark is just fading away. A break will break the monotony of the dull marriage that you are facing. Time will make you long for each other, and you will appreciate all the good times you had when you were with your partner. People notice the importance of things when they lose them. Therefore, creating an illusion of losing your partner is a guaranteed way to rekindle the spark. Hopefully, the rekindled spark will return you to your early dating days when you were inseparable.

Chapter 15:

Master the Art of Listening

Throughout this handbook, you have learnt the ultimate skill of communication. Now you'll get to tackle the most essential aspect of communication – listening.

Are you hearing what your spouse is saying, or are you listening? What's the difference between these two? Well, hearing is more of consuming words from someone's utters while listening involves comprehending and understanding what one is telling you.

In most cases, people just hear words without understanding; not due to language barrier or illiteracy, but due to either current emotions towards the person talking or certain feeling against the topic being discussed. It's not necessarily negative emotions or feelings. Sometimes, you may just be absent-minded, thinking about a non-related situation.

Without the skill of listening keenly, you find yourself either comprehending the wrong things, or getting lost in the conversation because you missed the important bits of it.

When it comes to marital arguments or conversations, listening to your spouse will help you understand their reasoning and their feelings. You'll be able to know why they did what they did, and it will save your marriage. Unfortunately, during arguments most people want to talk rather than listen. Keeping quiet and watching your spouse talk doesn't guarantee that you're listening. You might be thinking of a response as your spouse speaks, making you hear but not understand what's being said. This is because they walked into a conversation with an agenda in mind, and the ego to win the argument. The lack of listening skills is one of the reasons most arguments escalate, and spouses part ways.

That said, this chapter will guide you through the benefits of listening to your spouse, and equip you with the skill of listening.

Benefits of Listening to Your Spouse
Why is it important to listen to your spouse as they speak to you? Here are some benefits to note down.

You know what your spouse thinks of you

There is no other way to understand what your spouse thinks unless you give them a chance to talk. Allowing your spouse to talk will allow them to rant on and on about issues that affect them. While listening carefully, you can learn what the idea they have of you. It can be a good thing if they think of you positively but horrible if they think of you negatively. Whatever way you discovery goes, you will have the information you need and therefore use it to your advantage.

If she thinks of you negatively, you can, later on, correct her and inform her that you are on the same team and correct her where you think she could have been wrong about you. Knowing what they think about you will also enable you to understand the expectations they have of you and how you can manage them. It can guide you to know how to act in the future when different situations happen.

Fewer arguments

A lot of information passes when people communicate. Your spouse might be talking about the same things day in day out. But since you do not listen attentively, the information they are trying to relay may not be getting to you. They can be talking about their insecurities, fears, or criticizing some of your behaviour. When you pay attention and listen to what your partner has to say, you will know what irks and what pleases them. Knowing these two things is beneficial to you since it will be easier for you to predict how they act and out can change how they feel quickly.

When you know what partner hates, you should try as much as possible to avoid it since it is sure one of the main reasons for arguments. Choosing to take this action will cause fewer arguments in your marriage, and you can, therefore, have more peaceful and fun conversations instead. Listening also makes you understand how your partner talks. There will consequently be fewer conflicts due to more understanding.

It completes you

Women are different from men. Your spouse may be seeing things that you are not aware of. Women are known to have some intelligence, and men are known to have other qualities that women lack. Since both groups have a factor that the other is missing, you will only be complete when your spouse contributes their knowledge. This knowledge is readily available when you listen to what your partner has to say concerning different issues.

However, your spouse may not be right about everything they are saying. From the large amount of information that they give, it is your responsibility to pick out the relevant information to you and choose how you are going to use it to your advantage. When your spouse notices that the information they are offering to you is helpful and is doing you well, they can also decide to adopt a listening habit. In this way, both of you get to benefit.

Harmonious environment

When you listen to what your spouse says, you will have a peaceful environment. Failing to listen to your spouse can bring problems such as not knowing their preferences. If you are keenly listening to your spouse, you will know what she likes and how she likes it done. You will also be aware of your surroundings and get different opinions that you would not see. Following your spouse's preferences and what you learn about yourself is very important in shaping your environment. Incorporating your preferences and those you learn from your spouse about the environment you are living in will help you improve it. In the end, you will be in a harmonious environment where both of you are happy and satisfied.

Become a good spouse

There is no real or standard measurement of what makes a good spouse or a bad one. Everybody has their perspective of what they deem wrong and what they consider as good. Despite the different measures that people have to determine right and wrong, there are the universal ones that are agreeable with everyone. Listening is one of them. Everyone likes getting listened to, and being ignored makes everyone feel unloved and worthless. Therefore you need to listen to your spouse when the talk since it makes them feel loved and appreciated. Failure to listen comes with many difficulties. Embracing listening as your skill will put you a step closer to becoming a good partner to your significant other.

Shows love

COMMUNICATION SECRETS FOR A HEALTHY MARRIAGE

Listening to your partner shows that you love them. It shows that you care about what they think, and they are an essential person in your life. Putting aside your things to listen to your spouse shows that they are a priority in your life. It makes them feel that they are more important than anything else, and that is why you have put it aside to listen to them. When you listen, you are likely to offer solutions to her problems where possible. It is vital since it shows your partner that you want them to succeed, and that is why you are trying to offer them solutions. However, listening to your spouse does not mean blindly following what they have to say. You need to listen and be rational in making your decisions before implementing what they were saying.

You learn

Listening helps you to grow. Since childhood, we are taught to listen so you can learn. In all aspects of life, you have to listen. When you were a child, you listened to your teachers who helped you learn in school. When you are at the workplace, you listen to your manager and colleagues to learn more about the job. Therefore, listening to your spouse will guide you through marriage and help you grow.

JEAN-CLAUDE
LEVEQUE

Learning more about your spouse will help you to have a happy marriage where both of you enjoy it.

Better sex

Listening to what your spouse says about sex will guide you and what they like. You will know the things they want, the ones they do not, and the ones they would like to experiment with. Paying attention will make you know the things that you both enjoy so that you can do them more and what to avoid since they dislike it. Because you know what they may be willing to experiment on. You can give her suggestions on what she may be inclined to and that you are also interested in. It can open both of you up to a more exciting experience that can help to spice up your marriage. You should, therefore, sharpen your listening skills and see the changes it can bring to your sexual life.

10 Steps to Master the Art of Listening

To effectively listen to your spouse, you need to do the following;

Face them and Maintain Eye Contact

While you can demand your child to face you while you speak, it'll be impossible to do the same with your spouse without making them feel disrespected. Talking to someone as they scan the environment or browse their phones is quite irritating. It shows that they care less about the conversation – or about your feelings. Facing your spouse may not mean that you're fully concentrating; Maybe you're fantasizing and admiring their face. Looking around doesn't mean you're distracted; however, the chances are that something will catch your eye and divert your attention.

Maintaining eye contact is not a skill that many have. Some get too shy they can't look in one's eyes for more than two seconds. Some look at the lips and read them as they move in speech. This is not a complete set of listening skills, but it's the right start.

Relax, Be Present and Attentive
Now attend to your spouse. Relax your body and mind, and be ready to take in whatever's being said—being attentive means listening to each word and comprehending its meaning. Try and avoid thinking as they talk. Don't think about other things or about how you can interrupt them. Be present.

Have an Open Mind

As seen earlier, some people walk into a conversation with a made-up mind. This makes it so hard for a spouse to converse or defend themselves during an argument. You may have thoughts in your mind and a set of conclusions. However, a good listener gives the speaker a chance to change their thoughts. Not to influence blindly with sweet words, but to take note of facts and possibilities that were earlier unknown.

Do Not Interrupt your Spouse

Interrupting your spouse is not only rude, but also a sign of not listening. You hear a familiar word and jump into conclusions, literally with words thrown at them. When you're itching to respond, hold your horses, take a deep breath and keep listening to them. If they seem like they have completed their speech or they ask you a question and hand over the floor, then blurt your thoughts. However, think about those thoughts before saying them out loud. Also, don't try to impose solutions without listening to the full story.

Picture their Thoughts

If your spouse is trying to explain a scenario, try to

get graphical about it. Picture what they are saying
to see if it makes sense and understand deeper.
When you picture their thoughts, it'll be like you're
in their mind.

*Wait for them to Pause or End their Speech to Ask
Questions*
In case you have questions on what they have just
said, be patient and wait for a pause then ask
questions. Ever been in a situation whereby you
interrupt and ask a question, then the speaker says
that they were just about to explain that? This
shows your level of impatience.

Ask Follow up Questions to Understand Further
Asking questions shows your spouse that for one,
you're interested in understanding the story or
explanation and secondly, you're listening
attentively. Ensure to have some follow up
questions. These are also good for better
understanding. When it comes to explaining an
accusation, don't ask follow up questions in mockery
just to show them that they're foolish or so to
speak. Use a calm tone and polite wordings. On the
same note, give them ample time to respond to your
questions.

Try Paraphrasing to Attain Clarification

Sometimes you may want to paraphrase a sentence out loud to see if what your spouse said is what you've understood. Just like asking questions, it shows that you were attentive. This gives your spouse a chance to clarify what they said.

Put yourself in your Spouse's Shoes

As you listen to them and get their emotions, put yourself in their shoes and understand why they made such decisions. Sometimes remaining in your shoes prevents you from feeling the person's bruises. You analyze things as yourself instead of as being in their situation. As you do so, you may end up feeling empathy instead of anger.

Be an Active Listener and Give Regular Feedback

Nod your head for affirmations or shake your head. Respond with "hhhmmm", "uh huh", "yes", "true", and such like exclamations as they talk. These are not considered interruptions since they only show that you agree with what's being said and that you're following the story keenly. Also, laugh when they say something funny, or slightly smile, or frown when the story gets too sad.

Look Out for Non-Verbal Cues

You don't only listen to what's being said, but also what's being shown. Human beings show their emotions using non-verbal cues. These help you understand a situation better. Look at their body language as they fidget and shiver, move their limbs uncomfortably or scratch their heads occasionally. Read their facial expressions; are they frowning, smiling, or seem mentally distant. The most crucial non-verbal cue is tonal variation. How high is their tone when talking to you. Do they seem angry or excited? Tone can help you know how to handle your spouse effectively.

The ultimate skill in the art of listening, is patience. Be patient and wait for your spouse to finish what they are saying and by the end of their 'speech', you will realize that you've gained some level of understanding that you didn't have before the talk. Everyone wants to be heard and understood making the art of listening on its own (before even responding), a reason for reconciliation. When your spouse feels appreciated that much, then they will return the favour and even get more reasonable with the situation.

Listening is not only effective during arguments. Listen when your spouse is telling you a funny story, or when they are requesting simple favours. Listen as they relate with others, and this will help you understand their character better.

Five Ways to Be a Good Listener To Your Spouse

Would you like to be an extra-ordinary listener to your spouse? Here are a few tips for you.

Listen with empathy

When practising empathy, it means that you are putting yourself in your spouse's shoes so you can see things from their perspective. It involves letting go of what you think and fully listening to your partner to fully understand how they view the world and how that specific matter affects them. When listening with empathy, you do not get to choose if to listen to the exciting conversations and ignore the boring ones. You listen to all the conversations that your spouse brings and try to enjoy them as much as possible.

Listening helps you to get what is going on in their world, and if it is an argument they are trying to bring up, you can understand their views, and later on, you can base your point on what she said. When your spouse knows that you are listening to her, she gets the confidence to tell you everything she ever wanted to say to you. It will make it easy for her to open up and become vulnerable around you. It also shows her that you care about her and love her. And that is why you care about what she had to say.

You may tend to zone out when your significant other starts talking about specific topics that do not interest you. If you notice this as a problem on your part, try to focus. It can be in attempting to view the things they are talking about from their perspective. Trying to understand the impact of the things your spouse is talking about to their life will make you more empathetic to them. It will also help you to see the amount of pressure they are facing so that you can be of help where possible.

Listen for emotion

Talking about emotions can be very challenging. When your partner talks about an issue that affects them and is a very emotional matter, you are likely to get carried away. It happens because you start thinking about your own emotions and try to figure out how that issue affects you emotionally.

Based on how the matter affects you emotionally, you are likely to respond in a way that may be offensive to your spouse. Your intentions may be genuine, but the way you package the reaction by not considering how your partner feels may come off as offensive to your spouse. It can also be because you are trying to alleviate the pressure that comes with that emotion and in the process, go wrong. It may be because you did not put yourself in your partner's shoes, and you, therefore, do not know the seriousness of the emotion.

Take your time to listen to your partner and trying to understand the emotions they are feeling. It will help you to know the feeling to portray and also answer to their issues in the right way that will make them feel loved and appreciated. Controlling your emotions to match them to those of your spouse during communication is essential since it will help you focus on the conversation and give them the encouragement they need.

Listen without bias

You and your spouse are different people. Every individual has their thought process and how they perceive things. You are both allowed to have independent opinions. In some matters, you might be having the same opinion, but in others, it can be different. When communicating with each other, it is essential to set your ideas aside and listen to your spouse without judgment. Try to be neutral even during an argument. If you remain rigid on your opinion and your significant other also decide the same, all your discussions will end in a stalemate.

However, setting your opinions aside, you can listen to a matter critically and understand the issue from a different perspective. Ignoring your opinion while listening to your spouse is the only way you are going to listen empathetically and also be able to relate to their emotions. However, this does not mean that you change your opinion for the sole purpose of pleasing your spouse. It means that you should have an open mind while listening. It is because if you stick to your opinion on matters, you will ignore some information. If you ignore some details of the conversation, you will not fully understand what your spouse is saying. It also means that you should keep your opinion to yourself unless your spouse asks for it.

Listen lovingly

Communication is useful when the words match the body language. Therefore, when listening to your partner talking, you should try and show a loving body language. It shows your partner that you are listening and that they can be sure of your love no matter the situation they are going through. Body language can be expressible in many different forms.

However, you can choose the one you are most comfortable doing during the conversation. It can be simple eye contact, agreeing with a node, or smile. It will assure them that you are paying attention, and you care about what they are saying. Since they are someone you live, you should be comfortable to touch them in a reassuring way to show them that you love them and respect them. When your partner wants to talk about an issue that is bugging them, you need to stop what you are doing and turn to face them as they talk.

Sitting and leaving what you are doing to listen to them shows you enjoy talking to them. When you leave everything you were doing to listen to your spouse, they will feel loved and may even be inspired to do the same for you when you need a listening ear.

Listen generously

COMMUNICATION SECRETS FOR A HEALTHY MARRIAGE

Your spouse is the person who is most entitled to your time. Therefore when they need your time to listen to them, you need to be there. You may be having your busy schedules and deadlines you need to meet that may seem like a priority, but your spouse is also a priority to your life, and therefore, their time needs to be budgeted as well.

Creating time for your spouse will show them that you love them and care about what they say. Having the time designed for them, they will be free and go to depths to talk about their issues. From the problems they are talking about, you will know what affects them and how you can be of help on the matter. Given this opportunity, your spouse bound to feel loved and appreciated and, therefore, more confident when talking to you. They are also like to bring to you any issue bothering them in terms of fears, hopes, or concerns.

Conclusion

Thank you for making it through to the end of *Communication Secrets For A Healthy Marriage* let's hope it was informative and able to provide you with all of the tools you need to achieve your goals whatever they may be.

The next step is to have some personal time and meditate about your current marital situation. Are you in a healthy or unhealthy marriage, and does it seem to have a chance to rekindle the love? If your answer is negative, then it might be time to visit a therapist. It's never advisable to request or file for divorce when the slightest misunderstandings occur, else you may need one husband for every year of your life

Therefore, don't be a quitter, make an effort and put up a fight to save your marriage. Have options that would help your love stay strong and try them all with patience and positivity. A marriage full of frequent and good communication lasts because as spouses, you get to stay on the same page throughout this lifetime experience. Talking also helps strengthen your bond as a couple and helps you grow as individuals.

Communication comes with understanding and empathy. It also entails patience, honesty, and perseverance. Getting closure is essential not only to you, but to your spouse as well. Talking helps get rid of accumulated stress, worry, or pain in the heart. All the best as you take these detailed steps to improving communication in your marriage.

Finally, if you found this book useful in any way, a review on Amazon is always appreciated!

A Short message from the Author:

Hey, are you enjoying the book? I'd love to hear your thoughts!

Many readers do not know how hard reviews are to come by, and how much they help an author.

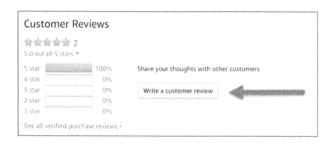

I would be incredibly thankful if you could take just 60 seconds to write a brief review on Amazon, even if it's just a few sentences!

You can leave a review under the Orders page, at the links below.

https://www.amazon.com/your-account
https://www.amazon.co.uk/your-account

Thank you for taking the time to share your thoughts!

Made in the USA
Las Vegas, NV
04 April 2022